SANDOR KATZ
AND THE
TINY WILD

WRITTEN BY Jacqueline Briggs Martin AND June Jo Lee
ILLUSTRATED BY Julie Wilson
AFTERWORD BY Sandor Katz

Readers
to **Eaters**

SAN FRANCISCO, CALIFORNIA

Readers
to **Eaters**

READERS to EATERS
1620 Broadway, Suite 6, San Francisco, CA 94109
readerstoeaters.com

Distributed by Publishers Group West
Printed in the USA by Worzalla, Stevens Point, WI (2/22)

Book design by Red Herring Design
Book production by The Kids at Our House
Special thanks to our co-editor, Gillian Engberg

The text is set in ITC Barcelona.

10 9 8 7 6 5 4 3 2 1
First Edition

Cataloging-in-Publication Data is on file at the Library of Congress
ISBN: 978-0-9980477-1-3

FSC
www.fsc.org

MIX
Paper from
responsible sources
FSC® C002589

Picture this:

In the woods of Middle Tennessee,
halfway up a tall, **TALL** hill
is a place called Walnut Ridge
where a green garden leads to
a log house, powered by sunshine.

Cross the **crickety-crockety** porch
into a kitchen full of curious people
tasting fizzy, funky, sometimes furry flavors.

And there is Sandor Katz
joyfully reaching inside a big jar
of salt-and-water brine,
fishing for pickled treasures—
flavor messages from the **tiny wild**.

Welcome to Sandor's fermentation school,
no desks, no tests, no standing in line,
mostly jars, chopping boards, and salt.
And, of course, cabbages and cucumbers,
all covered with the tiny wild
invisible microbes that change
cucumbers into crunchy dill pickles,
cabbages into **zingy-zangy** kimchi.

Fermentation

A no-heat cooking process in which microbes (microscopic organisms such as bacteria, yeast, and mold) transform vegetables and other raw ingredients into flavors we love

Kimchi

Spicy fermented vegetables
(from Korean, 김 KIM "immerse"
+ 치 CHI "vegetable")

SILVER PALACE 銀宮 TO GO

PICKLES

Sandor Ellix Katz grew up
in New York City, on the Upper West Side,
eating sauerkraut on hot dogs
and kosher dill pickles.

You could say the idea for Sandor's school
was sparked by pickles when he was a boy.
"I loved those sour, salty flavors," he said.

He loved pickles so much
he wandered the **mickety-mockety** streets
of the Lower East Side to find them
and even crossed the Brooklyn Bridge
to more pickle neighborhoods.

He thought he would live
in this dazzling city
forever.

Sauerkraut
Fermented cabbage
(from German, SAUER "sour"
+ KRAUT "herbs")

DELI & GROCERY

ICE · SANDWICHES · NEWS · COFFEE ·

I ♥ NY

HOT DOGS & SAUERKRAUT

As a young man, Sandor worked to build
city parks and waterfront walkways
that connected New Yorkers.

During this time, he saw friends become sick
with a mysterious new disease called AIDS.
Many died.

Eventually, scientists discovered
that AIDS was caused by the HIV virus.

In 1991, Sandor got tested for HIV
and learned that he had the virus, too.

This scary news changed him.
"I could no longer picture my future," he said.

DANDELIONS

Sandor read all he could about HIV,
AIDS, and how to take care of his body.

He worked less, slept more, ate more plants.
His yoga teacher showed him how to
forage for wild plants in Central Park.

Sandor said, "I wanted to get to know
plants better, grow plants,
and learn from plants in the wild."
Busy city life no longer felt good.

CENTRAL PARK

**GARLIC
MUSTARD**

BLACKBERRIES

MUGWORT

PURSLANE

SASSAFRAS ROOT

Sandor left New York City
to join a community of queer folks
in the woods of Middle Tennessee.

How would a New Yorker like Sandor
fit into life in the country?

Picture this:

Rickety-rackety houses, no-flush toilets,
solar panels for electricity, a barn for goats,
unruly gardens, berry bushes in the underbrush,
and no store for miles.

Here, everybody
made their own food, made their own fun.
They ate together, argued, and danced in drag
when the work was done.

Sandor milked goats: Sassy, Lentil, Luna.
He stressed less, gardened more,
foraged in the woods,
made salads and berry jam,
and felt better.

He said, "I could work in the garden
and my plant friends were there.
I could go walking in the forest
and my plant friends were there, too."

At times, he preferred the quiet of plants.
At times, he felt plants were his best friends.

One fall day, Sandor began to worry
about the cabbages in the garden.

They were all, **ALL** ready to harvest.
But no one wanted to eat cabbage
for breakfast, lunch, dinner, and snack.

How could Sandor keep good cabbage
from going to waste?

He remembered sauerkraut on hot dogs he ate as a kid.
Could he make his own kraut from cabbage?
He found a recipe and an old kraut crock in the barn.

Sandor chopped the cabbage,
added salt, kneaded, and squeezed
until cabbage juices made a salty brine.
He packed it all in the crock.

And waited. And waited.

PACK

SALT

-LICIOUS!!!

After a few days,
Sandor saw the fizzy bubbles,
smelled the funky fragrance,
tasted the salty sour crunch of kraut!
Kraut-e-licious!

The tiny wild Tennessee microbes
had fermented sweet cabbage into sour kraut.

The next time Sandor mixed cabbage and salt,
he spiced it with kimchi dazzle—
garlic, ginger, chili—
to make super-delicious kraut-chi!
Kraut-chi-licious!

Kraut-chi
German sauerkraut with
Korean kimchi spices

He loved the funky garlicky taste so much
he served kraut-chi with family meals,
gave kraut-chi to friends, took kraut-chi to potlucks.
Friends called him Sandorkraut.

ZINGY

ZANGY

Then, he tried making kosher dills.
But his first try, MUSHY!
So, he tried again. And again.
Until finally, CRUNCHY!
Pickle joy!

Fermenting foods felt good in his new life.
Fermented foods felt good
    in his body.

KRAUT
CHI!

YAY
SANDOR
KRAUT!

BEES

RULE!

INJERA
Ethiopia

LASSI
India

TEMPEH
Indonesia

MISO
Japan

In his Tennessee kitchen,
Sandor made lacy Indian dosa crepes,
spongy Ethiopian injera flatbread,
creamy Afro-Brazilian acarajé fritters.

TORSHI
Persia

SOURDOUGH BREAD
Europe / USA

PICKLES
Russia

KIMCHI
Korea

PUTO
Philippines

DOSAS
India

Sandor realized the tiny wild was worldwide.
People everywhere used old family recipes
to no-heat cook with microbes.

SAUERKRAUT
Germany

DOUCHI
China

红茶菌

红茶菌

KOMBUCHA
China

Sandor wrote a book—*Wild Fermentation*—
then loaded a pick-up truck with
forty gallons of kraut-chi,
and drove off to bookstores and food stores
to share his love of fermented foods.

Crowds learned to make kraut-chi
with Sandor's easy no-rules plan:
Chop, salt, squeeze, pack, and wait.
Chop it chunky. Chop it fine.
"Chopper's choice!" he said.

Sandor's new fermenting friends
sent him questions, and also invitations
to visit Panama, Estonia, Tasmania,
and other faraway places.

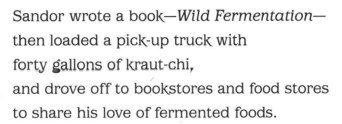

SMILE, YOU ARE IN ESTONIA

DEAR
SANDOR,
Come visit
US in China!
We love you!
X X O

KRAUT CHI
FOREVER!

Welcome
To
PANAMA

JUNIPER
BERRIES

nel seeds

CHILI
PEPPER
FLAKES

SALT

CORIANDER
SEEDS

Wild
Ferment
ation
SANDOR
KATZ

KRAUT
CHI

In China, Sandor learned a new-old way to make pickles.

Mrs. Ding made her pickles
in a sweet saltwater brine
she started years ago—
as long as she added fresh vegetables,
the fermentation continued.

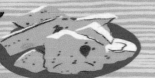

Sandor loved the idea of reusing brine
to make new pickles.
Nothing lost or wasted.
A perpetual brine!

Back home, Sandor started
his own perpetual brine.
Old brine, new vegetables
kept the tiny wild bubbling
at Walnut Ridge, too.

From China to Middle Tennessee,
Sandor sees fermentation as
how we are in the world:
always changing,
not just taking, but adding back,
kraut-chi-ing our way,
making new out of old.

Fermentation is a magical bridge
that connects all, **ALL**—
people, plants, and the tiny wild.

Will you join us at Sandor's kraut-chi school?
Will you make kraut-chi?

2 Add a small handful of salt.

SALT

3 Knead and squeeze until the cabbage is juicy.

6 Burps and bubbles will tell you the tiny wild is cooking.

In a few days you will have your own kraut-chi. Share YOUR delicious dazzle with the world!

A NOTE FROM SANDOR KATZ

Sandor Katz and a jar of kraut-chi

Hey kids!

I hope that reading this book got you thinking about microbes, because they are everywhere!

Microorganisms are all over us, inside us, and around us. We cannot see them, because they are so small (microscopic), but there are very many of them, and their importance is huge.

People, animals, plants, and all other forms of life rely upon microbes in many different ways. We get nourishment from the food we eat with the help of microbes, and they help maintain and protect our health. In similar ways, microbes in the soil help plants to grow.

The collection of microbes that is part of each of us is called our microbiome. In each person, our microbiome will be a little different, depending upon where we live, what we eat and drink, and our daily activities. In our human microbiome, as in the soil where our food is grown, diversity makes for health.

You can encourage microbe diversity in your gut by eating lots of different vegetables. Vegetables are not only delicious, but also full of vitamins, special nutrients related to their bright colors, and fibers, all great for your gut microbes.

You can also bring greater biodiversity to your gut bacteria by eating delicious, healthy fermented foods like yogurt and sauerkraut.

As you get older, try to learn about food. Help your family with the cooking (and the cleaning). Maybe even try your hand at fermenting, foraging for wild foods, or gardening.

I wish you many delicious microbes!

Sandor Katz

June Jo Lee and Sandor Katz

Jacqueline Briggs Martin

A Note from Jacqueline Briggs Martin

One reason I love writing books is that I learn so much while I am working on them. And that was especially true for this book. I learned a lot from working with June Jo Lee. She is a wonderful observer and notices patterns and small details. And she knows how to ask just the right questions—of people and of our writing.

I also learned more about fermenting vegetables. And I have shared what I learned with my family, many of whom now eat what they call "magic cabbage" every day. But the most important thing I learned—to my surprise—is that fermenting vegetables is a lot like writing. Both involve a process—a beginning (chopped cabbage and vegetables or an idea), some mixing (salt with the cabbage, more details/more ideas), a waiting period. With cabbage and vegetables, the mix just sits, and the microbes make the change; with writing, we have to keep working, keep revising.

And of course, there can be failures. Sandor Katz failed in his first batch of pickles. He started again. When a piece of writing doesn't work—too long, too short, too hard to understand—we have to start again. But we do, because we love pickles, or we love the story we are trying to tell. And both pickles and good stories put smiles on our faces. Here's to fermenting—vegetables and ideas.

JACQUELINE BRIGGS MARTIN is the author of many children's books, including *Snowflake Bentley*, winner of the Caldecott Medal. *Sandor Katz and the Tiny Wild* is part of her award-winning "Food Heroes" series, which includes *Farmer Will Allen and the Growing Table, Alice Waters and the Trip to Delicious,* and *Chef Roy Choi and the Street Food Remix,* which she co-authored with June Jo Lee. She lives in Mount Vernon, Iowa. jacquelinebriggsmartin.com

A Note from June Jo Lee

I love the funky super-delicious kraut-chi flavor of sour pickles and old kimchi. Sandor Katz taught me that Korean kimchi is German sauerkraut, and Jewish pickles are Korean pickles. He showed me that we are all connected to each other through our love of kraut-chi making, kraut-chi foods, and kraut-chi flavor.

I am a food ethnographer who studies and writes about how, what, and why we eat. For this book, I conducted fieldwork in May 2018 at Sandor Katz's Fermentation School in his Walnut Ridge home. As I stepped into his kitchen, I smelled the very familiar garlicky funky fragrances I grew up with in Korea. I heard joyful, upbeat sounds of people from all over the world chatting and chopping cabbages, of onions sizzling and kimchi stew bubbling in hot cast iron pots. And there he was (!) with his deep blue eyes, big mustache, and an arm inside a crock.

He told us, "I always like learning from my students." And for the next seven days, we tasted and made fermented foods, swapped stories, ate together, and laughed together. By the time we left Walnut Ridge, we were all transformed—livelier, funkier, and more wild.

This story about Sandor Katz is a four-year "fermentation" writing project with my co-author, Jacqueline Briggs Martin. We took "raw" ethnographic interviews with Sandor, mixed in our own experiences making kimchi and kraut, and added a dash of dazzle—words, rhythms, and images—to spice it up. As two cooks in the kitchen, we had so much fun kraut-chi-ing our way to write this book. I hope you try your hand at writing and fermenting something delicious with a friend, too.

JUNE JO LEE is a food ethnographer, studying how America eats for Google and other organizations. She co-founded Readers to Eaters, a publisher promoting food literacy through stories about our diverse food cultures. She also co-authored *Chef Roy Choi and the Street Food Remix,* a 2018 Robert F. Sibert Honor Award for best informational book. She lives in San Francisco. foodethnographer.com

JULIE WILSON has created billboards in New York City's Times Square and on the Sunset Strip in Los Angeles; painted murals at Coney Island; and produced many editorial illustrations for magazines and newspapers. Her artwork has been heavily influenced by TV cartoons and Pop Art. She lives in Santa Monica, California, where she works in a garage with the big door open, the sun shining in, and music or old movies playing in the background. This is her first picture book. juliewilsonillustration.com

More About the Tiny Wild

Microbes (we call them "tiny wild" in this book) are microscopic organisms that include bacteria, viruses, and fungi (such as yeasts and molds). "Wild" microbes are all around us—in the air, in the soil, on the plants we eat. Microbes inside our intestines (our microbiome) help us break down food into the nutrients our bodies need to live. Microbes in the soil digest old leaves, branches, and other organic materials into nutrients needed for gardens and forests to grow.

Common microbes (Lactobacillus, yeasts, and molds) transform vegetables, fruits, beans, grains, and dairy into new flavors, textures, and aromas. This transformative process of no-heat cooking by microbes is called fermentation. For thousands of years, people around the world have been preserving the harvest by making fermented foods such as pickles, sourdough bread, chocolate, cheese, sauerkraut, and kimchi. These foods have a lot of umami, often described as savory, earthy, deep, and rich mouth-feel. We like to call this super-delicious fermented flavor "kraut-chi."

More About Sandor Katz

Sandor Katz is the bestselling author of many books including *The Art of Fermentation*, which won a James Beard Foundation Book Award in 2013. Through his writing and workshops, Sandor shares his love for the transformative power of microbes to make delicious fermented foods.

Sandor was 29 years old in 1991 when he tested HIV positive, before there were effective treatments. HIV (human immunodeficiency virus) is a microbe that causes AIDS (acquired immune deficiency syndrome). He now takes medicines to control HIV. While there is still no cure for HIV-AIDS, these drugs help HIV-positive people live healthier, longer lives.

In 1993, Sandor joined an LGBTQ+ community in Middle Tennessee. The community is off the grid! No electrical power, municipal water, or industrial foods. Residents raise goats, grow their own vegetables, cook their own meals, and maintain a collaborative DIY (do-it-yourself) way of life. The fermentation workshops that Sandor started in his Walnut Ridge home now attract students from all over the world.

Selected Books by Sandor Katz

2003 *Wild Fermentation: The Flavor, Nutrition, and Craft of Live-Culture Foods* (Vermont: Chelsea Green)
2006 *The Revolution Will Not Be Microwaved: Inside America's Underground Food Movements* (Vermont: Chelsea Green)
2012 *The Art of Fermentation* (Vermont: Chelsea Green)
2020 *Fermentation as Metaphor* (Vermont: Chelsea Green)
2021 *Sandor Katz's Fermentation Journeys* (Vermont: Chelsea Green)

Selected Resources

ARTICLES
Bilger, Burkhard, "Nature's Spoils: The underground food movement ferments revolution." *The New Yorker*, July 21, 2014

Halberstadt, Alex, "Out of the Woods." *The New York Times Magazine*, August 6, 2015

ONLINE VIDEOS
"Sandorkraut: A Pickle Maker." *The New York Times*, July 29, 2015

Botto, Mattia Sacco, with Sandor Katz. "People's Republic of Fermentation // Episode 01: Mrs. Ding's Pickles." *YouTube*, 3:33-11:30, July 1, 2017

ETHNOGRAPHIC FIELDWORK
(conducted by June Jo Lee)
Participant-observation with Sandor Katz and students at the Fermentation Residency Workshop at his Walnut Ridge home in Tennessee (May 2018); while eating pickles from Zabar's at Riverside Park in New York City (January 2019); and while foraging and feasting in the woods of Sandor's Tennessee (October 2020).

For more resources, visit the book's webpage: readerstoeaters.com/our-books/sandor-katz-and-the-tiny-wild